Lewis Carroll first told the story of *Alice in Wonderland* to Alice Liddell and her two sisters while on a boating trip on the river Thames. Alice was bored and asked him to tell a story 'with lots of nonsense in it'. In his story, he used objects and places that they had seen in their outings around Oxford that summer. Alice was enchanted by the story, and asked him to write it down for her.

Read all the Classic Adventures

A Little Princess
The Wind in the Willows
The Railway Children
Treasure Island
Black Beauty
Peter Pan
Heidi

Lewis Carroll's

Alice in Wonderland

Adapted by SUSAN HOLLIDAY

Illustrated by Alan Marks

First published as *Alice's Adventures in Wonderland*
in Great Britain in 1865

This adaptation published in 2001 for WHSmith,
Greenbridge Road, Swindon, SN3 3LD
by Hodder Children's Books

10 9 8 7 6 5 4 3 2 1

A Catalogue record for this book is available from the British Library

ISBN 0 340 85277 1

Typeset by Avon Dataset Ltd, Bidford-on-Avon, Warks

Printed and bound in Great Britain by
The Guernsey Press Co. Ltd, Channel Isles

Hodder Children's Books
a division of Hodder Headline Limited
338 Euston Road
London NW1 3BH

Contents

1

Down the rabbit-hole

It was a lazy summer's afternoon. Alice sat by her elder sister on the grassy bank and yawned. She was very bored! It had been a long day.

She rubbed her sleepy blue eyes and peered at the book her sister was reading. But there were no pictures in it or people talking.

And what's the use of a book like that! she thought. She pushed back her long, fair hair and put a daisy behind her ear. Then she held the daisy under her tilted nose. But there was no smell. Then, just as she was making up her mind to make a daisy chain, to her surprise, a White Rabbit with pink eyes ran close by her. She thought she heard the Rabbit saying to himself, 'Oh, dear! Oh, dear! I shall be too late.'

Alice blinked. The rabbit took a watch out of his waistcoat pocket, looked at it, then hurried on. Without knowing why, Alice got up. She found herself running across the field after him. She was just in time to see him pop down a large rabbit-hole under the hedge.

Without thinking about how to get out again, Alice followed the Rabbit into the hole.

Down, down, down she fell into what seemed to be a well. Either it was very very deep, or she fell very very slowly, for she had plenty of time to look about her. The sides of the well were filled with cupboards and book shelves. Maps and pictures hung on pegs. Now she was passing a jar labelled ORANGE MARMALADE! Alice loved marmalade so she stretched out her hands and picked it up.

'It's empty,' she said crossly, 'what's the use of that?' So she put it back into another cupboard as she fell past.

Down, down, down she went.

After this, she thought to herself, I won't think anything of falling downstairs! By now I must be getting somewhere near the centre of the earth. I wonder what latitude or longitude I've reached?

(She liked saying words like that even when she had no idea what they meant.)

I wonder if I shall fall right *through* the earth? she went on. I shall have to find out what the name of the country is. And she imagined herself asking: 'Please, miss, is this New Zealand or Australia?'

Down! Down! Down! Would the fall never

end? To pass the time Alice began to think of her cat.

Dinah will miss me very much tonight, she thought. I hope someone remembers to put out her saucer of milk!

As she went on thinking of her cat she began to feel sleepy, and said to herself, in a dreamy sort of way. 'Do cats eat bats? Do bats eat cats? Do cats eat bats . . . ?'

She was almost asleep when suddenly, with a great thump, the fall was over!

Alice wasn't a bit hurt, and in next to no time she jumped up and looked round. Above her it was dark but in front of her was a long passage and there was the White Rabbit hurrying down it! Alice followed him as fast as she could. As he turned the corner she heard him say, 'Oh my ears and whiskers, it's getting late, it's getting late!'

By the time Alice reached the corner the rabbit was nowhere to be seen. She was now in a long, low hall lit up by a row of lamps hanging from the roof. There were doors round the walls but they were all locked. Then she caught sight of a little three-legged table, made of solid glass. A tiny golden key was placed on it. She tried all the doors but none of them opened. Then she came across a curtain she hadn't seen before and behind it was a little door nearly half a metre high. She tried the little golden key and to her surprise it fitted!

She opened the door and looked inside. A tiny passage, not much larger than a rat-hole, led into the loveliest garden she had ever seen. If only she could run round the bright flower-beds and in and out of the cool fountains! But she couldn't even get her head through the doorway!

And even if my head *did* go through, she thought, it wouldn't be much use without my shoulders!

So she went back to the table and now she found a little bottle on it labelled: DRINK ME.

She wasn't going to do *that* in a hurry!

'I'll look first,' she said, 'and see if it's marked *poison*.'

But it wasn't so she opened the bottle and tasted the drink. It was very nice – a sort of mixed flavour of cherry tart, custard, pineapple, roast turkey, toffee and hot buttered toast. She soon drank it all up.

'What a strange feeling,' said Alice, after a while. 'I think I'm getting smaller and smaller!' To her surprise she was now only twenty-five centimetres high! She waited for a few minutes to see if she was going to shrink any further but nothing happened.

Now I can go out into the garden, she thought, but she'd forgotten the little golden key! When she went back to the table she was far too small to reach it. She tried her best to climb up one of the legs of the table, but it was too slippery. She went on trying until she was so tired she sat down and cried.

'Stop crying!' she told herself. 'Don't be silly!'

As she calmed down, she saw a little glass box lying *under* the table. Inside was a very small cake with the words EAT ME marked out in currants.

'I'll eat it,' said Alice boldly. 'If it makes me taller, I'll be able to reach the key and if it makes me smaller, I'll creep under the door. Either way I'll get into the garden.'

She ate some of the cake then held her hand on top of her head to feel which way she was growing. She was quite surprised to find she was the same size.

'Never mind, I'll go on eating it,' she said and it wasn't long before she had finished off all the cake.

2

The pool of tears

'How strange it all is!' cried Alice. 'I seem to be getting taller and taller. My neck's nearly as long as a giraffe's! I can't even see my feet. Goodbye feet!'

At that moment her head struck the roof of the hall. She was now about three metres high! She picked up the little golden key and hurried off to the garden door. She lay on one side and looked at the garden with one eye. But she was far too big to get through. It all seemed so hopeless she sat down and began to cry again. But it was not long before she told herself off. 'You ought to be ashamed of yourself, Alice. A great girl like you, crying in this way! Stop at once!'

But she didn't stop and she shed gallons of tears, until there was a pool all round her, about ten centimetres deep, that reached halfway down the hall.

After a time she heard a little pattering of feet in the distance. She quickly dried her eyes to see who was coming. It was the White Rabbit on his way back. He was very smartly dressed, and was carrying a pair of white gloves in one hand and a large fan in the other. Alice could hear him muttering to himself, 'Oh! The Duchess, the Duchess! Oh! Won't she be cross if I've kept her waiting.'

'If you please, sir –' said Alice. The Rabbit was so startled he dropped the white gloves and the fan, and ran away into the darkness as fast as he could go.

Alice picked up the fan and gloves. The hall was very hot so she kept fanning herself and thinking how strange everything was.

Did I change in the night? she wondered. Let me think! Was I the same when I got up this morning? Can I still remember things?

She tested herself by reciting a rhyme she thought she knew well:

'How does the little crocodile
Improve his shining tail,
And pour the waters of the Nile
On every golden scale?

'How cheerfully he seems to grin,
How neatly spread his claws,
And welcome little fishes in
With gently smiling jaws!'

'They're not the right words!' she said to herself. 'Everything's different down here.'

It was true! When she looked down at her hands she was surprised to see she had put on one of the Rabbit's little white gloves.

How *can* I have done that? thought Alice. I must be growing small again.

To make sure, she got up and stood next to the table to measure herself by it.

'Another change!' she said. 'I must be about sixty centimetres high by now. And I'm still shrinking fast!' It must be the fan I'm holding, she thought and dropped it quickly, just in time to avoid shrinking away altogether.

'That *was* a narrow escape!' she said, and ran as fast as she could back to the little door. But it was shut again and the little golden key was lying on the glass table just as it had been.

Things are worse than ever, thought Alice. I've never been as small as this before, never!

As she said these words her foot slipped and in another moment, splash! she was up to her chin in salt water. She was in the pool of tears which she had wept when she was about three metres high.

'I wish I hadn't cried so much!' she said to herself.

Just then Alice heard something splashing about in the pool a little way off.

She swam towards the sound and found it was a mouse who had slipped in like herself.

'Oh, Mouse!' she said. The Mouse looked

at her with curiosity. He seemed to wink at her with one of his little eyes, but he said nothing.

Perhaps he doesn't understand English, thought Alice. I expect he's a French mouse, come over with William the Conqueror.

So she began again in French: '*Où est ma chatte*?' (This means: *Where is my cat*. It was the first lesson in her school French book.)

The Mouse leapt out of the water and shook all over with fright.

'I *am* sorry,' cried Alice, 'I forgot mice don't like cats!'

'Not *like* cats!' cried the Mouse in a shrill voice. 'Would *you* like cats if you were me?'

'Well, perhaps not,' said Alice gently. 'Don't be angry about it. If I could show you my cat Dinah you might think differently. You might take a fancy to cats if you could only see her. She sits purring ever so happily by the fire, licking her paws and washing her face. She's such a nice soft thing to cuddle and she's so good at catching mice . . . Oh, I'm sorry!'

The Mouse bristled and Alice looked worried. 'We won't talk about Dinah any more if you'd rather not.'

The Mouse trembled down to the end of his tail. 'As if I would talk on such a subject! Our family have always hated cats. Nasty, low, common creatures! Don't let me hear that word again!'

'Of course not,' said Alice, and she tried again. 'Are you – are you fond – of – of dogs?'

At this the Mouse swam away as quickly as he could go.

Alice called softly after him, 'Dear Mouse! Do come back again, and we won't talk about cats or dogs either, if you don't like them!'

When the Mouse heard this, he turned round and swam slowly back to her.

His face was quite pale and he said in a low trembling voice, 'Let's get to the shore and then I'll tell you why I hate cats and dogs.'

By now it was high time to go! The pool was getting very crowded with birds and animals that had fallen into it. There was a Duck and a Dodo, a Parrot and an Eaglet, and several other strange creatures.

Alice led the way and the whole party swam to the shore after her.

3

A Caucus-race and a long tale

They were an odd-looking party as they stood together on the bank, dripping wet, cross and uncomfortable. The first question was how to get dry again. Because of this Alice found herself talking to the animals and birds as if she had known them all her life. She had quite a long argument with the Parrot, who in the end turned sulky, and would only say, 'I'm older than you and *must* know better.'

Alice wanted to know how old he was, but the Parrot refused to tell her so there was no more to be said.

At last the Mouse, who seemed to be the leader of the party, called out: 'Sit down, all of you, and listen to me. *I'll* soon make you dry enough!'

They all sat down at once, in a large ring, with the Mouse in the middle. Alice hoped he would come up with an answer. She felt sure she would catch a bad cold if she didn't get dry very soon.

'Ahem!' said the Mouse with an important air, 'are you all ready? This is the driest thing I know. Silence all round, if you please!' Then he began to tell them all about William the Conqueror. After a while he said to Alice, 'How are you getting on now, my dear?'

'As wet as ever,' said Alice. 'Talking about William the Conqueror doesn't seem to dry me at all!'

'In that case,' said the Dodo solemnly,

rising to his feet, 'I move that the meeting adjourn.'

'Speak plain English!' said the Eaglet. 'I don't know the meaning of those long words and I don't believe you do either.' The Eaglet bent down her head to hide a smile while some of the other birds giggled.

'What I was going to say,' said the Dodo in an offended tone, 'was, that the best thing to get us dry would be a Caucus-race.'

'What's a Caucus-race?' said Alice.

The Dodo peered at her. 'The best way to explain it is to do it.'

First he marked out a race-course, in a sort of circle, and then he placed the animals and birds along the course, here and there, without very much thought. There was no 'ONE TWO THREE GO!' as there usually is. Instead everyone began to run when they liked, and left off when they liked, so it wasn't easy to know when the race was over. However, when they had been running half an hour or so, and were quite dry again, the Dodo suddenly called out, 'The race is over!' They all crowded round, panting and asking, 'Who has won?'

The Dodo sat for a long time with one finger pressed on his forehead. He thought very hard indeed. At last he said: '*Everybody*'s won and everybody must have prizes.'

'But who's going to give the prizes out?' they asked together.

'*She* is, of course,' said the Dodo, pointing to Alice with one finger. At this, everyone crowded round her and called out: 'Prizes! Prizes!'

It was all very confusing and Alice had no idea what to do. In despair she put her hand in her pocket and pulled out a box of sweets. There was exactly one each!

'But *she* must have a prize herself, you know,' said the Mouse.

'Of course,' the Dodo replied gravely and he turned to Alice. 'What else have you got in your pocket?'

'Only a thimble,' said Alice sadly.

'That will do,' said the Dodo. 'Give it to me!'

Everybody crowded round Alice while the Dodo solemnly presented her with the thimble. He made a short speech and they all cheered.

The next thing was to eat the sweets! This caused a lot of noise and confusion but when everyone had finished eating, they sat down again in a ring, and begged the Mouse to tell them something more.

'Mine is a long and a sad tale!' said the Mouse.

'It's a long tail, certainly,' said Alice, looking down in amazement at the Mouse's tail, 'but why do you call it sad?' Alice's mind wandered and she found herself imagining how the Mouse's tale (tail) would go:

Fury said to a
mouse, that he
met in the
house,
'Let's both go to
law: *I* will
prosecute
you! Come!
I'll take no denial –
We must have a trial
for really this morning
I've nothing to do.'
Said the mouse to the cur,
'Such a trial,
dear sir,
with no jury
or judge
would be
wasting
our
breath.'
'I'll be judge,
I'll be jury,'
said cunning old Fury,
'I'll try
the whole
cause
and
condemn
you
to
death!'
and
so
on
. . .
.

'You're not listening to me!' said the Mouse crossly to Alice. He stood up, looking very offended, and walked away.

'Please come back and finish your story!' called Alice but the Mouse only shook his head impatiently and walked a little quicker.

'What a pity he wouldn't stay!' sighed the Parrot, as soon as the Mouse was out of sight, while an old Crab said to her daughter, 'Ah, my dear! Let this be a lesson to you never to lose *your* temper.'

'I wish I had our Dinah here,' said Alice aloud, to no one in particular. 'She'd soon bring back the Mouse!'

'And who is Dinah, if I might be so bold as to ask the question?' said the Parrot.

'Dinah's our cat,' said Alice, 'and she's brilliant at catching mice. What's more, she'll eat a little bird as soon as look at it!'

At this some of the birds hurried off at once. One old Magpie began wrapping itself up very carefully, saying, 'I really *must* be getting home! The night air doesn't suit my throat!' Then a Canary called out in a trembling voice to its children, 'Come away, my dears! It's high time you were all in bed!'

Soon they all moved off and Alice was left on her own.

'I wish I hadn't mentioned Dinah!' she said to herself sadly. She began to cry again, for she felt very lonely.

In a little while, however, she heard a pattering of footsteps in the distance.

4

The Rabbit sends in a little bill

It was the White Rabbit, and Alice heard him muttering to himself, 'The Duchess! The Duchess! Oh, my fur and whiskers! She'll get me executed, as sure as ferrets are ferrets! Where can I have dropped them, I wonder?'

Alice guessed he was looking for the fan and the pair of white gloves, so she began hunting about for them. But everything seemed to have changed since her swim in the pool. The great hall, with the glass table and the little door, had vanished completely.

Very soon the Rabbit noticed Alice, and called out angrily.

'Why, Mary Ann, what are you doing out here? Run home this moment and fetch me a pair of gloves and a fan!'

Alice was so frightened she ran away. Soon she came to a neat little house. On the door was a bright brass plate with the name 'W. RABBIT' engraved upon it. She went inside and found her way into a tidy little room with a table at the window. On it was a fan and two or three pairs of tiny white gloves. As she picked them up she saw a little bottle near the mirror.

'I'll just see what this bottle does,' she said. 'I do hope it'll make me grow large again.'

She uncorked it and put it to her lips. Before she had drunk half the bottle, she found her head pressing against the ceiling and soon she had to kneel down on the floor! She went on growing and growing. In the end she had to put one arm out of the window, and one foot up the chimney. Luckily for Alice the little magic bottle had finished working. She stopped growing

and after a few minutes heard a voice outside.

'Mary Ann! Mary Ann! Fetch me my gloves at once!'

The Rabbit pattered upstairs and tried to open the door. But he couldn't get in and muttered to himself, 'I'll go round and climb in the window.'

After a while Alice heard a little shriek and a fall and a crash of broken glass.

'Pat! Pat! Where are you?' shouted the Rabbit angrily and an unknown voice replied, 'Sure then I'm here! Digging for apples, yer honour!'

'Digging for apples, indeed!' said the Rabbit angrily. 'Come and help me out of this cucumber frame. And tell me, what's that in the window?'

'Sure, it's an arm, yer honour!'

'An arm, you idiot? Well, it's got no business there, at any rate. Go and take it away!'

There was a long silence.

Alice spread out her hand and made a snatch in the air. There were two little shrieks and more sound of broken glass.

I wonder what they'll do next, she thought. As for pulling me out of the window, I only wish they *could*!

At last she heard a rumbling of little cart-wheels and the sound of voices talking together. She made out the words: 'Here, Bill! The master says you're to go down the chimney.'

I wouldn't be in Bill's place for all the world! thought Alice. This fireplace is narrow but I can still *kick* a little!

She drew her foot as far down the chimney as she could, gave one sharp kick, and waited to see what would happen next.

The first thing she heard was a general chorus of 'There goes Bill!' and then the Rabbit's voice alone – 'Catch him, hold up his head . . . Brandy now . . . How was it old fellow?' And then a little, squeaking voice: 'No more, thank ye; I'm better now!

All I know is, something comes at me like a jack-in-a-box and up I goes like a rocket!'

The next moment a shower of little pebbles came rattling in at the window. Some of them hit Alice in the face. 'You'd better not do that again,' she shouted.

Outside there was a dead silence.

Alice noticed with some surprise that the pebbles that lay on the floor were all turning into little cakes.

If I eat one of them, she thought, it's sure to make some change in my size. So she swallowed one and to her delight began to shrink straight away.

As soon as she was small enough she rushed out of the house and found quite a crowd of little animals and birds waiting outside. They all made a dash for her so she ran off as fast as she could, and was soon safely hidden in a dense wood.

The first thing I have to do is to grow to my right size again, she thought. The second thing is to find my way into that lovely garden I saw through the little door.

While she was peering between the trees, a little sharp bark overhead made her look up. An enormous puppy was looking down at her with large round eyes. He stretched out a paw and tried to touch her. Hardly knowing what she did, Alice picked up a little stick and held it out. The puppy jumped into the air and rushed at the stick, while Alice dodged behind a great thistle to keep herself from being run over. The puppy kept charging at the stick until he grew tired and sat down again, a good way off, panting, with his tongue hanging out of his mouth and his great eyes half shut.

As soon as Alice saw the puppy was snoozing she ran on and on until his bark was only a faint sound in the distance. She leaned against a buttercup and fanned herself with one of the leaves.

'He was a dear little puppy,' she said. 'I would have loved to teach him tricks! If – if only I'd been the right size!'

She looked round. There was a large mushroom growing nearby, about the same height as herself. Alice stretched up on tiptoe and peeped over the edge of the mushroom. Her eyes immediately met those of a large blue caterpillar. It was sitting on the top with its arms folded, quietly smoking one of those long pipes called a hookah and taking no notice of her or of anything else.

5

Advice from a caterpillar

The Caterpillar and Alice looked at each other for some time in silence. Then the Caterpillar took the hookah out of its mouth and spoke to Alice in a sleepy voice.

'Who are *you*?'

Alice replied shyly, 'I don't really know, sir, not at the moment.'

'What do you mean?' said the Caterpillar sternly. 'Explain yourself!'

'I can't explain myself,' said Alice,

'because I'm not myself, you see.'

'I don't see,' said the Caterpillar. '*You*! Who are you?'

'I'm not sure,' said Alice, 'I keep changing size. It's very muddling!'

'No it's not,' said the Caterpillar.

Alice was annoyed with the way he replied.

'I think you ought to tell me who you are first,' she said.

'Why?' said the Caterpillar.

What's the point of talking to him? thought Alice. We're just going round and round in circles. So she turned to go.

'Come back!' said the Caterpillar. 'I've something important to say.'

Alice tried not to feel cross and turned back.

Keep your temper!' said the Caterpillar.

'Is that all?' said Alice, trying very hard not to be angry.

The Caterpillar puffed away, then took the hookah out of its mouth and said, 'So you think you've changed, do you?'

'I'm afraid I have, sir,' said Alice. 'I change size all the time and I can't remember things like I used to.'

'Recite *You Are Old, Father William,*' said the Caterpillar.

Alice folded her hands and began:

' "You are old, Father William," the young man said,
"And your hair has become very white;
And yet you continually stand on your head –
Do you think, at your age, it is right?"

"In my youth," Father William replied to his son,
"I feared it might injure the brain;
But, now that I'm perfectly sure I have none,
Why, I do it again and again!" '

'I'm afraid it's not quite right,' said Alice, timidly.

'It's wrong from beginning to end,' said the Caterpillar.

They were silent for a while, then the Caterpillar spoke.

'What size do you want to be?'

'I'd like to be bigger,' said Alice. 'It's not very nice being very small.'

'You'll get used to it,' said the Caterpillar. It yawned several times and shook itself. Then it slid down the mushroom.

'Listen to me,' it said. 'One side of this mushroom will make you smaller and the other side will make you taller.' With that it crawled away into the grass.

Alice broke two pieces of mushroom, one from either side. She nibbled at the right-hand bit. Almost straight away she felt a violent blow. Her chin had struck her foot! She was frightened of the sudden change and tried to eat some of the other bit. Her chin was pressed so closely against her foot that there was hardly any room to open her mouth. But at last she managed to swallow a morsel of the left-hand piece. Now all she could see, when she looked down, was an immense length of neck, which seemed to rise like a stalk out of a sea of green leaves. Her neck bent this way and that, like a serpent's. She was about to dive in among the leaves – which turned out to be the top of the trees, when a sharp hiss made her draw back in a hurry. A large pigeon flew into her face and beat her violently with its wings.

'Serpent!' screamed the Pigeon.

'I'm *not* a serpent,' said Alice.

'Yes you are,' said the Pigeon. 'It's hard enough hatching eggs without being on the lookout for serpents all the time. I haven't had a wink of sleep for three weeks.'

'I'm *not* a serpent,' said Alice. 'I'm a – I'm a little girl.'

'Do you expect me to believe you?' said the Pigeon. 'I've seen a good many little girls in my time, but never one with a neck like that. No! You're serpent. I suppose you'll be telling me next that you've never tasted an egg!'

'Of course I've tasted eggs,' said Alice.

'Then I know what you're doing,' said the Pigeon. 'You're looking for eggs. Anyway, it doesn't matter to me whether you're a little girl or a serpent!'

'It matters to *me*!' said Alice quickly. 'And as it happens, I'm not looking for eggs. And if I was, I wouldn't want *yours*. I don't like them raw.'

'Well go away, then,' said the Pigeon in a sulky voice, as it settled down again into its nest.

After a while Alice remembered that she still held the pieces of mushroom in her hands, so she started to nibble first one, then the other. Sometimes she grew taller and sometimes she grew shorter. At last she brought herself down to her usual height.

It took her a few minutes to get used to this. 'How strange all these changes are,' she said to herself. 'I'm never sure what I'm going to be, from one minute to another! But at least I'm back to my right size.' Then she remembered the little garden and sighed. 'I would love to go there, but I've no idea how I can.'

She walked on and soon came across an opening in the wood where there was a little house, just over a metre high.

I'm so big, thought Alice, I'd be really frightening to anyone who lives there.

So she began to nibble at the right-hand bit of mushroom and didn't go anywhere near the house until she was a lot smaller.

6

Pig and pepper

For a minute or two Alice stood in front of the house, wondering what to do. Suddenly a footman ran out of the wood, looking like a fish! He was wearing a special livery uniform, with a powdered wig on his head. He knocked loudly on the door. It was opened by another footman who looked like a frog! He was also wearing livery and had a powdered wig on his head. What strange creatures, thought Alice.

She crept a little way off to listen to what they were saying. The Fish-Footman handed a huge letter to the Frog-Footman.

'It's for the Duchess,' he said gravely. 'It's an invitation from the Queen to play croquet.' Then he hurried away.

The Frog-Footman sat on the ground near the door, staring stupidly at the sky.

Alice went up to the door and knocked.

'It's no use knocking,' said the Frog-Footman. 'I'm the same side of the door as you are! Anyway, they're making such a noise inside no one will hear you'.

It was true! Unbelievably loud sounds came from inside. There was a constant howling and sneezing and every now and then a great crash, as if a dish or kettle had been broken to pieces. Suddenly the door opened and a large plate skimmed out and grazed the Footman's nose. There was more howling and sneezing and crashing from inside the house and the door banged shut again.

'What am I to do?' said Alice.

'Anything you like,' said the Footman. 'I shall sit here, on and off, for days and days.' And he began whistling.

It's no good talking to him, thought Alice, he's as daft as they come.

So she opened the door and went into a large kitchen that was full of smoke. The Duchess was sitting on a stool in the middle of the room, nursing a baby, while the cook leaned over the fire, stirring a large saucepan full of soup. There was so much pepper in the soup that everyone was sneezing except the cook and a large cat who was sitting on the hearth, grinning from ear to ear.

Alice turned to the Duchess. 'Could you tell me why your cat grins?'

'It's a Cheshire cat,' said the Duchess, 'that's why.'

'I didn't know cats could grin,' said Alice.

'They all can,' said the Duchess, 'and most of them do.' Then she turned to the baby and shouted, 'PIG!'

The cook took the saucepan off the fire and began to throw everything she could at the Duchess and the baby. Fire-irons, saucepans, plates and dishes crashed about! The Duchess took no notice but the baby howled so much, Alice couldn't help crying out, 'Please be careful!'

'If everyone minded their own business,' said the Duchess, 'the world would go round much faster.'

'That wouldn't help,' said Alice, and she began to show off. 'The earth takes twenty-four hours to turn round on its axis—'

'Talking of axes,' said the Duchess, 'chop off her head.'

Alice looked anxiously at the cook to see if she would take the hint; but the cook went on stirring the soup as if she had heard nothing. So Alice went on: 'Twenty-four hours, I think, or is it twelve?'

'Don't bother me!' said the Duchess, 'I never could stand numbers!' She began nursing her child again and shaking him at the end of every line as she sang:

'Speak roughly to your little boy,
And beat him when he sneezes:
He only does it to annoy,
Because he knows it teases.'

While the Duchess sang the second verse she tossed the baby up and down so violently that the baby howled loudly. Alice could hardly hear the rest of the song.

'I speak severely to my boy,
I beat him when he sneezes;
For he can thoroughly enjoy
The pepper when he pleases.'

The Duchess looked at Alice. 'Here, you take the baby. I have to play croquet with the Queen.'

Alice just about managed to catch the child. If I don't take him away, she thought, something dreadful might happen! So she carried the baby into the wood. He was a funny-looking creature, like a starfish with arms and legs waving about. Alice examined him closely. He had a nose like a snout and very small eyes, like a pig. He grunted again, and this time Alice realised that he *was* a pig!

This won't do! she thought, so she put him down and watched him trot quietly away into the wood. Then she looked up and was startled to see the Cheshire Cat grinning from the bough of a tree, a little way ahead.

'Cheshire Puss,' said Alice with respect, for the cat had lots of teeth and very long claws, 'could you tell me where I should go from here?'

'It all depends on where you want to go,' said the Cat.

'I don't mind as long as I go somewhere,' said Alice. 'What sort of people live round here?'

The Cat waved its right paw. 'Over there lives a Hatter.' Then it waved its left paw. 'And over there lives the March Hare. They're both mad. We're all mad here. I'm mad, you're mad—'

'How do you know?' said Alice.

'You must be,' said the Cat, 'or you wouldn't be here.' It licked its paws and looked up again. 'Are you playing croquet with the Queen today?'

'I'd like to,' said Alice, 'but I haven't been invited.'

'You'll see me there,' said the Cat and immediately vanished. Then it reappeared.

'By the way, what happened to the baby?'

'He turned into a pig,' said Alice.

'I thought he would,' said the Cat and vanished again.

Alice waited for a while, half expecting to see it again. She was right! Just as she was making up her mind to visit the March Hare the Cat came back again!

'Did you say pig, or fig?' it asked.

'Pig,' said Alice, 'and I'm getting very dizzy with you coming and going so quickly.'

'All right,' said the Cat. This time it vanished slowly, beginning with its tail and ending with its grin.

I've seen a cat without a grin, thought Alice, but I've never before seen a grin without a cat!

Soon she came to the March Hare's house. The chimneys were shaped like ears and the roof was thatched with fur. It was so large she ate some more of the left-hand bit of mushroom until she was about sixty centimetres high. She walked slowly up to the house. She felt rather afraid. Maybe she should have gone to see the Hatter instead!

7

A mad tea-party

The March Hare and the Hatter were having tea at a table under a tree, in the front garden. A dormouse lay between them and they were using him as a cushion, resting their elbows on him and talking over his head.

Although the table was large they were all crowded together in one corner.

'No room! No room!' they cried.

'There's lots of room,' said Alice and sat

in a large armchair at the other end of the table.

'Would you like some wine?' asked the March Hare.

Alice could only see a pot of tea. 'I can't see any,' she said.

'There isn't any,' said the March Hare.

'Then why did you offer it?' said Alice.

'Why did you sit down without being invited?' said the March Hare.

'I didn't know it was *your* table,' said Alice, and there are lots of places laid.'

'Your hair needs cutting,' said the Hatter.

'That's a very personal thing to say,' said Alice.

Instead of replying the Hatter opened his eyes very wide and said, 'Why is a raven like a writing desk?'

'I like riddles,' said Alice eagerly, 'I think I know the answer.'

'Do you mean you can find it out?' said the March Hare.

Alice nodded. 'That's the same thing, isn't it?'

'Don't be an idiot,' said the Hatter, 'you might just as well say I see what I eat is the same as I eat what I see!'

They sat in silence until the Hatter said, 'What's today?'

'The fourth,' said Alice, after a while.

'Two days out,' said the Hatter. 'I said butter wouldn't suit the works!' He looked angrily at the March Hare who now took out his watch.

Alice looked at it over his shoulder.

'That's a funny watch,' she said. 'It tells the date but it doesn't tell the time.'

'Why should it?' said the Hatter and changed the subject.

'The Dormouse is asleep again,' he said. 'I'll pour some hot tea on his nose.'

'Just what I was going to say,' said the Dormouse, with his eyes shut.

'Have you guessed the riddle yet?' asked the Hatter.

'I give up,' said Alice, 'what's the answer?'

'I've no idea,' said the March Hare. 'By the way, have you ever spoken to Time?'

Alice was puzzled. 'Well, no. But I've learned how to beat time to music.'

'There you are!' said the Hatter. 'Time doesn't like being beaten. If you kept in his good books he'd do anything for you. For instance, if it was time to go to school, he'd make it lunch-time. Just like that!'

'I only wish it was,' said the March Hare gloomily.

The Hatter shook his head. 'The trouble is I had a quarrel with Time. It was last March – just before *he* went mad –' he pointed to the March Hare. 'It was at a concert given by the Queen of Hearts. I had to sing:

'Twinkle, twinkle, little bat,
How I wonder what you're at!
Up above the world you fly,
Like a tea-tray in the sky.'

'I just finished the first verse when the Queen shouted out: "He's murdering the time. Off with his head!" Ever since then Time won't do what I ask. It's always six o' clock now.'

'Is that why there are all these tea things?' said Alice.

'That's it,' sighed the Hatter. 'It's always tea-time and we've no time to wash the cups and plates in between.'

'I suppose you keep moving round the table instead,' said Alice.

'That's it!' said the Hatter.

'But what happens when you're at the beginning again?'

But now the March Hare was tired of the subject and asked the Dormouse to tell a story. So the Dormouse began: 'Once upon a time there were three little sisters called Elsie, Lacie and Tillie. They all lived together at the bottom of a well—'

'What did they live on?' asked Alice.

'Treacle,' said the Dormouse.

'Didn't it make them ill?' said Alice.

'Very ill,' said the Dormouse.

'That's a bit silly,' said Alice. 'Why did they live at the bottom of a well?'

'Because it was a treacle well.'

'No such thing,' said Alice.

'Do *you* want to finish the story?' said the Dormouse crossly.

'Please go on,' said Alice and the Dormouse continued. 'The three sisters were learning to draw treacle.'

'I want a clean cup,' interrupted the Hatter. 'Let's move round.'

So everybody moved. The Dormouse followed the March Hare, and Alice sat in the March Hare's seat. Only the Hatter was better off. Alice was far worse off than before, because the March Hare had spilt milk into his plate.

The Dormouse went on with his story, even though he was yawning and rubbing his eyes.

'They were learning to draw,' he said

sleepily, 'they drew all sorts of things beginning with M.'

'Why M?' asked Alice.

'Why not?' said the March Hare.

The Dormouse muttered sleepily, 'Mouse-traps, moon, memory, muchness – you know, much of a muchness. Have you ever seen a drawing of muchness?'

'Of course not,' said Alice.

'Then stop talking,' said the Hatter.

I'm not putting up with this rudeness, thought Alice and she walked away.

She turned round once or twice, half hoping they would call her back. But the Dormouse had gone to sleep and the March Hare and the Hatter were trying to put him into the teapot.

What a silly tea-party, thought Alice. Never again.

She made her way through the wood until she came to a tree that had an odd little door in the trunk.

'Everything here's a bit strange,' said

Alice, out loud, to give herself courage. 'I might as well go in.'

She went through the door and there she was back in the long hall, beside the glass table. She picked up the little golden key and unlocked the door that led into the garden. 'I'll get there this time,' she said as she nibbled at the mushroom she had kept in her pocket. Soon she was the right height and could walk down the little passage. At last she was in the beautiful garden. She ran round the bright flower beds and went in and out of the cool fountains.

8

The Queen's croquet-ground

'What a lovely rose tree,' said Alice as she stood at the entrance of the garden.

Three gardeners, who all looked like playing cards, were painting the roses red.

'Look out now, Five!' one of them was saying. 'Don't go splashing paint over me like that!'

'I couldn't help it,' said Five sulkily. 'Seven jogged my elbow.'

'That's right, blame others!' said Seven.

'*You* can talk!' said Five. 'I heard the Queen say only yesterday *you* deserve to be beheaded.'

Seven flung down his paint brush. 'That's not fair!'

Suddenly they all caught sight of Alice and bowed low, as if she was a queen.

'Could you tell me why you're painting the roses?' she asked.

It was Two who spoke. 'This should have been a red rose tree. If the Queen finds out it's white, we'll all have our heads cut off. So we're painting the roses, before she comes.'

He no sooner spoke than the Queen appeared. The three gardeners instantly threw themselves flat on their faces and Alice turned round to see the royal procession.

First came ten soldiers carrying clubs and looking like playing cards. Next came ten courtiers in clothes decorated with diamond patterns walking two by two like the soldiers. After them came ten royal children in costumes covered with hearts and then the guests who were mostly kings and queens.

'And there's the White Rabbit,' exclaimed Alice. He was followed by the Knave of Hearts who carried the King's crown on a crimson velvet cushion. Last of all came the King and Queen of Hearts.

When the procession reached Alice, everyone stopped and looked at her.

'Who's this?' said the Queen.

'I'm Alice, Your Majesty,' she said, then added under her breath, 'They're only a silly pack of cards. There's nothing to be afraid of.'

'And who are these?' asked the Queen, pointing to the three gardeners who were lying on their fronts and looked like the rest of the pack of cards.

'I haven't a clue,' said Alice, 'and it's nothing to do with me!'

The Queen turned red with anger. 'Off

with her head!' she screamed.

'Nonsense!' said Alice loudly and the Queen was silent.

'She's only a child,' said the King timidly, while the Queen shouted to the three gardeners, 'Get up, all of you.'

The gardeners jumped up straight away and bowed to everyone.

'Stop that,' said the Queen, 'it makes me giddy.' Then she had a close look at the roses. 'So that's what the gardeners have been doing! Off with their heads!'

'You shan't be beheaded,' Alice told the gardeners and put them into a large flower-pot that stood nearby. The procession moved on except for three soldiers who wondered about looking for the gardeners.

'Are their heads off yet?' shouted the Queen.

'Their heads are gone, Your Majesty,' the soldiers shouted back.

'*You*!' shouted the Queen to Alice. 'Can you play croquet?'

'Yes!' shouted Alice.

'Come on then!' roared the Queen.

Alice wondered what was going to happen next. She walked next to the White Rabbit who told her in a frightened whisper, 'The Duchess is going to be executed!'

'What for?' asked Alice.

'She boxed the Queen's ears.'

Alice couldn't help laughing.

'Sshh,' whispered the Rabbit, 'she'll hear you.'

But now the Queen was shouting, 'Come along! Find your places!' and everybody ran around until the game began.

What a funny croquet-ground, thought Alice. It's all uneven! The balls are live hedgehogs, the mallets live flamingos and the soldiers are bent in two like arches so the balls can run through them! I've never seen anything like it!

She had great trouble with her own flamingo mallet. When she straightened it

out to hit one of the hedgehog balls it twisted its head round and looked at her face. She couldn't help laughing! And then there were the players who all played at once without waiting for their turn! They fought over the hedgehog balls and all the time the Queen kept shouting furiously, 'Off with his head! Off with his head!'

It's a wonder anyone's left alive, thought

Alice uneasily. She longed to escape but at that moment she saw something that really puzzled her, so she stayed to look at it.

It was a grin, hanging in the air. Then she remembered the Cheshire Cat.

Now I'll have someone to talk to, she thought. Very soon the Cat's head appeared round the grin and Alice said, 'It's nice to see you, Cheshire Cat. This is the most unfair game I've ever seen.'

'How do you like the Queen?' said the Cat in a low voice.

'I don't,' said Alice, 'She's so –'

She noticed the Queen was close behind her so she went on, '– likely to win, it's hardly worth finishing the game.'

The Queen smiled and went on.

'Who are you talking to?' asked the King.

'The Cheshire Cat,' said Alice.

The King put out his hand. 'He may kiss it if he likes.'

'I'd rather not,' said the Cheshire Cat.

'Don't look at me like that!' said the King.

'A cat may look at a king,' said Alice.

'Maybe, but—' said the King.

The Queen had only one way of settling arguments. 'Off with its head,' she said, without even looking round.

Alice thought she might as well see how the game was getting on. But her flamingo had flown to the other side of the garden and by the time she had caught it, the game was over. She tucked the bird under her arm so it wouldn't escape and went back to talk to the Cheshire Cat. To her surprise, a large crowd had gathered round it. The Executioner, the King and the Queen were all arguing together.

'*You* settle the argument,' they said to Alice.

'What's it about?' she asked.

'I can't cut off a head if there's no body,' said the Executioner.

'Nonsense!' said the King.' If there's a head, it can be beheaded.'

'If something's not done soon,' screamed

the Queen, 'I'll have *everyone* beheaded!'

'Why don't you ask the Duchess,' said Alice, who could think of nothing else to say.

'Fetch her!' said the Queen to the Executioner. 'She's in prison.'

But there was no need. The Cat's head was fading away and soon it had disappeared altogether.

The King and the Executioner ran wildly up and down looking for it, while the rest of the party went back to the game.

9

The Mock Turtle's story

'You can't think how glad I am to see you again, you dear old thing,' said the Duchess. She tucked her arm into Alice's and they walked off together.

Perhaps it was the pepper that made her so cross in the kitchen, thought Alice. Maybe pepper always makes people bad-tempered. Maybe vinegar makes them sour, camomile makes them bitter and barley-sugar makes them sweet.

The Duchess squeezed up to her. 'You've forgotten to talk,' she said, 'you're thinking so much.'

Alice hated being near the Duchess. She was very ugly and was resting her sharp chin on Alice's shoulder. But she didn't want to be rude so she said: 'The game's getting better and better, isn't it?'

'That's right,' said the Duchess. 'And the moral is: it's love that makes the world go round.'

Why does she go on about morals? wondered Alice.

'I'd put my arm round your waist,' said the Duchess, 'only I don't trust your flamingo. Flamingos and mustard both bite. The moral is: birds of a feather flock together.'

'But mustard isn't a bird!' said Alice. 'I think it's a mineral. Oh no! It's a vegetable. It doesn't look like one, but it is.'

'You're right as usual,' said the Duchess, 'and the moral of that is: be what you are.'

What a strange person the Duchess is, thought Alice.

'Thinking again?' said the Duchess, with a dig of her sharp little chin.

'I've a right to think,' said Alice sharply.

'Just as much right as pigs have to fly,' said the Duchess. 'The moral is—'

But she never finished her sentence for there was the Queen in front of them, with her arms folded and frowning like a thunderstorm.

The Duchess spoke in a low, weak voice. 'It's a fine day, Your Majesty.'

The Queen stamped and stormed. 'I'm warning you! Either you or your head must be off, and that's in half an hour's time. Take your choice!'

The Duchess took her choice and was gone in a moment.

'Let's get on with the game,' said the Queen to Alice. Alice was too frightened to say a word and followed her slowly back to the croquet-ground.

The other guests, who had been resting in the shade, hurried back to the game, but the Queen quarrelled with them all the time. 'Off with his head!' she shouted. 'Off with his head!' Soon everyone except the King, the Queen and Alice were either detained or put under sentence of death.

Suddenly the Queen stopped shouting and said to Alice, 'Have you seen the Mock Turtle yet?'

'No!' said Alice. 'What's a Mock Turtle?'

'It's the thing you make Mock Turtle Soup from,' said the Queen. 'He'll tell you his story.' As they walked off the King said to everyone in a low voice, 'You are all pardoned.'

That's good! thought Alice.

They soon bumped into a creature called the Gryphon who was lying fast asleep in the sun.

'Get up!' said the Queen. '*You* must take Alice to the Mock Turtle and *I* must get back to see if my orders have been carried out.'

The Gryphon watched the King and Queen until they were out of sight, then he chuckled.

'They never execute anyone, you know. Come on!'

They hadn't gone far before they saw the Mock Turtle, a little way off, sitting sad and lonely on a little ledge of rock, sighing as if his heart would break.

Alice pitied him deeply.

'What's the matter with him?' she asked the Gryphon.

'It's all make-believe,' said the Gryphon. 'He's not really sad you know.'

As they drew near, the Mock Turtle looked at them with large eyes full of tears.

'This here young lady wants to know your story,' said the Gryphon.

The Mock Turtle spoke in a deep, hollow voice. 'Sit down and don't speak a word until I've finished.' He paused. 'Once I was a real Turtle.' Then he was silent and Alice was about to say 'Thank you for an interesting story,' when he began again.

'When we were little,' said the Mock Turtle, sobbing now and then, 'we went to school in the sea. The master was an old Turtle, but we used to call him Tortoise—'

'Why did you call him Tortoise if he wasn't one?' said Alice.

'We called him Tortoise because he taught us,' said the Mock Turtle angrily. 'You're very dull.'

'You ought to be ashamed of yourself for asking such a simple question,' said the Gryphon. They both sat silently looking at Alice who felt ready to sink into the earth. At last the Gryphon said to the Mock Turtle: 'Drive on, old fellow! Don't be all day about it.' So the Mock Turtle went on:

'Yes, we did! We went to school in the sea, though you may not believe it—'

'I never said I didn't,' said Alice quickly for she didn't want to be told off again.

'We had the best of educations,' said the

Mock Turtle, 'in fact we went to school every day—'

'I've been to a day-school too,' said Alice hurriedly.

'With after-school subjects?' asked the Mock Turtle a little anxiously.

'Yes,' said Alice. 'We have French and Music Club.'

'And Washing?' asked the Mock Turtle.

'Of course not,' said Alice.

'Then yours isn't a really good school,' said the Mock Turtle in relief. 'Now at *ours* we had after-school French, Music and Washing.'

'You couldn't have needed much washing,' said Alice, 'living at the bottom of the sea.'

The Mock Turtle sighed. 'My parents couldn't afford anything extra. I just did the usual things.'

'What were they?' said Alice.

'Reeling and Writhing, of course,' said the Mock Turtle, 'and then different sorts of

Arithmetic – Ambition, Distraction, Uglification and Derision.'

'What's Uglification?' asked Alice.

The Gryphon lifted up both its paws in surprise. 'You've never heard of uglifying? You know what to beautify is, I suppose?'

Alice nodded.

'Well then,' went on the Gryphon, 'if you don't know what to uglify is, you're downright stupid.'

Alice didn't like his reply so she turned back to the Mock Turtle.

'What else did you learn?'

'There was Mystery, Ancient and Modern, Seaography, Drawling, Stretching and Fainting in Coils.'

'What was that like?'

'*I'm* too stiff to show you and the Gryphon never learnt it.'

'I went to the Classics Master though,' said the Gryphon. 'He taught Laughing and Grief, as they used to say.'

Alice tried to change the subject.

'How many hours a day did you do lessons?'

'Ten hours the first day,' said the Mock Turtle, 'nine the next, and so on.'

'How strange,' said Alice.

'That's why they're called lessons,' said the Gryphon, 'because they lessen from day to day.'

Alice thought hard. 'Then the eleventh day must have been a holiday?'

'Of course,' said the Mock Turtle.

'And what about the twelfth?'

'That's enough about lessons,' said the Gryphon, 'tell her about the games.'

10

The Lobster Quadrille

The Mock Turtle sighed deeply and drew one of his flappers across his eyes. He looked at Alice and tried to speak, but sobs choked his voice.

'It's the same as if he had a bone in the throat,' said the Gryphon and began to shake and punch the Mock Turtle. At last the Mock Turtle found his voice and with tears running down his cheeks, went on: 'You may not have lived at the bottom of the sea –'

'I haven't,' said Alice.

'And you've never met a lobster?'

'I once tasted—' began Alice, then added loudly, 'No, never!'

'I see,' said the Mock Turtle, 'so you can't imagine how nice it is to do a Lobster Quadrille?'

'No I can't,' said Alice. 'What sort of dance is it?'

'First of all you line up along the sea shore,' said the Gryphon.

'Two lines,' cried the Mock Turtle. 'Seals, turtles, salmon and so on. Then when you've got rid of all the jelly-fish you go two steps forward—'

'With a lobster for a partner,' shouted the Gryphon excitedly.

'Then one step forward,' screamed the Mock Turtle, 'change lobsters, then –'

'Throw the lobsters in the air!' shouted the Gryphon, jumping up and down.

'As far out to sea as you can,' cried the Mock Turtle. 'Swim after them, somersault –'

'Then change lobsters again,' yelled the Gryphon.

The Mock Turtle dropped his voice. 'Then back to land again.'

The two creatures, who had been jumping about like mad, sat down again very sadly and quietly and looked at Alice.

'Would you like to try it?' said the Mock Turtle.

'Yes please,' said Alice.

'We can do without lobsters,' said the Mock Turtle, 'but one of us must sing!'

'You sing,' said the Gryphon, 'I've forgotten the words.'

They began solemnly dancing round and round Alice while the Mock Turtle sang very slowly and sadly:

' "Will you walk a little faster?" said a whiting to a snail,
"There's a porpoise close behind us and he's treading on my tail.
See how eagerly the lobsters and the turtles all advance!
They are waiting on the shingle – will you come and join the dance?
Will you, won't you, will you, won't you, won't you join the dance?
Will you, won't you, will you, won't you, won't you join the dance?

"You can really have no notion how delightful it will be
When they take us up and throw us, with the lobsters, out to sea!"
But the snail replied. "Too far, too far!" and gave a look askance –
Said he thanked the whiting kindly, but he would not join the dance.
Would not, could not, would not, could not, would not join the dance.
Would not, could not, would not, could not, could not join the dance.'

'Thank you,' said Alice, glad it was over. 'And I like the song about the whiting.'

'Do you know why it's called a whiting?' said the Gryphon.

'Why?' said Alice.

'It does the boots and shoes,' said the Gryphon solemnly. 'Under the sea they're done with whiting. Now you know.'

'What are sea boots and shoes made of?' said Alice.

'Soles and eels, of course,' said the Gryphon, 'any shrimp could have told you that. Now – you tell us some of *your* adventures.'

'I could tell you my adventures from this morning,' said Alice, 'but not from yesterday. I was different then.'

She told them about the first time she saw the White Rabbit and how she couldn't remember *You Are Old, Father William*.

'Recite something now,' said the Mock Turtle.

The two creatures stood very close to her, one on either side.

'Recite *It's the Voice of the Sluggard*,' said the Gryphon.

Alice stood up but the words that she sang didn't seem to be the right ones.

> *'It's the voice of the Lobster; I heard him declare,*
> *"You have baked me too brown, I must sugar my hair."*

As a duck with its eyelids, so he with his nose,
Trims his belt and his buttons, and turns out his toes.'

'What nonsense!' said the Mock Turtle.

Alice put her face in her hands. Would anything ever come out right again?

'About his toes,' said the Mock Turtle, 'how could he turn them out with his nose?'

'She can't explain it,' said the Gryphon, 'she'd better give up.' He turned to Alice. 'Would you like the Mock Turtle to sing you another song?'

'Yes *please,*' said Alice.

The Mock Turtle sighed deeply and in a voice sometimes choked with sobs, began to sing:

'Beautiful Soup, so rich and green,
Waiting in a hot tureen!
Who for such dainties would not stoop?
Soup of the evening, beautiful Soup!

Soup of the evening, beautiful Soup!
Beau – ootiful Soo – oop!
Beau – ootiful Soo – oop!
Soo – oop of the e – e – evening,
Beautiful, beautiful Soup!'

The Mock Turtle was about to sing the second verse when a cry went up.

'The trial's beginning!'

'Come on,' cried the Gryphon, and taking Alice by the hand, he hurried her off.

Alice was soon out of breath. 'What trial is it?' she panted.

But the Gryphon only ran faster and faster and the Mock Turtle's singing was carried faintly on the breeze.

'Soo – oop of the e – e – evening,
Beautiful, beautiful Soup!'

11

Who stole the tarts?

The King and Queen of Hearts were seated on their throne surrounded by all sorts of birds and beasts, as well as the whole pack of cards: the Knave was standing before them, in chains, with a soldier guarding him on either side. The White Rabbit was next to the King with a trumpet in one hand and a scroll of paper in the other. Alice looked hungrily at the dish of tarts on the table in the middle of the court.

I wish they'd hurry up and finish the trial, she thought, so we could eat them all up.

But there was no chance of this so she passed the time looking round at the court. She had never been in a court of justice before, but she'd read all about them so she

knew who was who. He's the judge, she thought, pointing to the King. But fancy wearing a crown over his wig! And there's the jury-box with twelve jurors. But look, they're all made up of animals and birds. 'And why are they writing on their slates *before* the trial's begun? Can you tell me?' she whispered to the Gryphon.

'They're writing down their names in case they forget them,' said the Gryphon in a low voice.

'Stupid things!' said Alice loudly but she quickly stopped when the White Rabbit cried out: 'Silence in the court!'

One of the jurors (it was Bill the Lizard) had a pencil that squeaked and Alice couldn't bear it. She managed to slip behind him and take it away. Bill the Lizard couldn't make out what had happened. After this he wrote with one finger for the rest of the day, even though it left no mark on the slate.

'Herald, read the accusation,' cried the

King. The White Rabbit blew three blasts on the trumpet, unrolled the scroll and read out:

'The Queen of Hearts, she made some tarts,
All on a summer day:
The Knave of Hearts, he stole those tarts,
And took them quite away!'

'Call the first witness,' said the King.

It was the Hatter. He came in with a teacup in one hand and a piece of bread and butter in the other.

'You ought to have finished,' said the King. 'When did you begin?'

'Fourteenth of March, I think it was,' said the Hatter.

'Fifteenth,' said the March Hare.

'Sixteenth,' said the Dormouse.

The jury wrote down all three dates, added them up and, to Alice's surprise, gave the answer in pounds and pence.

It was at this moment that Alice realised she was growing again!

I'll stay until there's no more room for me, she thought.

'I wish you wouldn't squeeze me,' said the Dormouse, who was next to her. 'I can hardly breathe.' And he crossed the court.

'I can't help it,' said Alice, 'I'm growing!'

'You've no right to grow here,' said the Dormouse. All this time the Queen was staring at the Hatter. He trembled so much he shook off both his shoes.

'I'm a poor man, Your Majesty,' he said, in a trembling voice, 'and I hadn't begun my tea – not above a week or so – and what with the bread and butter being so thin – and the twinkling of the tea –'

'The twinkling of the what?' said the King.

'It began with the tea,' the Hatter replied.

'Of course twinkling begins with a T,' said the King. 'Get on with it!'

The poor Hatter dropped his teacup and bread and butter and went down on one knee. 'I'm a poor man, Your Majesty!'

'You're a very poor speaker,' said the King.

At this one of the guinea-pigs cheered so the court officers put him into a large canvas bag, head first, and then sat on it.

'If that's all you know, you may stand down,' said the King.

'I can't go no lower,' said the Hatter, 'I'm on the floor as it is.'

'Then you may sit down,' the King replied.

'I'd rather finish my tea,' said the Hatter, with an anxious look at the Queen.

'You may go,' said the King, and the Hatter left the court in such a hurry, he forgot to put on his shoes.

'Take off his head outside!' ordered the Queen, but the Hatter was out of sight before the officer could get to the door.

'Next witness!' said the King.

It was the Duchess's cook who arrived with the pepper-pot in her hand.

'Give your evidence,' said the King.

'Shan't,' said the cook.

The King frowned at her. 'Tell me, what are tarts made of?'

'Pepper, mostly,' said the cook.

'Treacle,' said a sleepy voice from behind.

'Behead that Dormouse,' shrieked the Queen. 'Turn him out of court. Pinch him! Off with his whiskers!'

For some minutes the whole court was in confusion as they turfed out the Dormouse. By the time everyone had settled down again, the cook had disappeared.

'Never mind!' said the King. 'Call the next witness!'

Alice wondered who the next witness might be. They haven't got much evidence yet, she thought. She could hardly believe it when the White Rabbit read out, at the top of his shrill little voice, the name, 'Alice!'

12

Alice's evidence

'Here I am!' cried Alice, jumping up. She forgot how large she had grown in the last few minutes and in her confusion at being called as a witness she tipped over the jury-box with the edge of her skirt. All the jurors fell on the heads of the crowd below. 'I'm *so* sorry,' she said and picked up the little birds and animals as quickly as she could.

'The trial can't go on,' said the King gravely, 'until all the jurors are back in their proper places.' He looked hard at Alice. '*All* of them.' Alice realised that she had put the Lizard upside down into the jury-box so she took him out again and put him back the right way up.

As soon as the jurors had recovered their slates and pencils, they began to write down what had happened to them. But the Lizard was too disturbed to write anything. He sat with his mouth open, gazing at the roof of the court.

'Do you know anything at all about trials?' the King asked Alice.

'Nothing at all,' said Alice.

'That's very important,' said the King and he kept whispering, 'Important, unimportant,' as if he was trying out the best word.

'Don't you mean unimportant?' said the White Rabbit.

'Of course: *unimportant*,' said the king.

Some of the jurors wrote down 'important' and others wrote down 'unimportant'.

'Whatever does it matter?' said Alice to herself.

Then the King shouted 'Silence!' and read out from his note-book.

'Rule Number Forty-two. Anyone who's more than a mile high is to leave court.'

Everybody looked at Alice.

'You're nearly two miles high!' said the Queen.

'That's not a real rule,' said Alice. 'You invented it just now.'

'It's the oldest rule in the book,' said the King.

'Then it ought to be Rule Number One,' said Alice.

The King turned pale. 'Think about your verdict,' he said to the jury.

At this the White Rabbit jumped up. 'We haven't yet examined this letter, Your Majesty. It's written by the prisoner to – to –' He looked up. 'There's no name on it. In fact, it's not a letter at all. It's a poem.'

'Is it in the prisoner's handwriting?'

asked one of the jury.

'No, it's not,' said the White Rabbit.

'Then he must have copied someone else's handwriting,' said the King.

'Please Your Majesty,' said the Knave, 'I didn't write the poem and no one can prove I did. I haven't signed my name.'

'That's dishonest,' said the King.

'And it *proves* you're guilty,' said the Queen.

'That's not true,' said Alice. 'Anyway, you don't know what the poem's about.'

'Then read it,' said the King.

The White Rabbit opened the piece of paper and read:

'They told me you had been to her,
And mentioned me to him:
She gave me a good character,
But said I couldn't swim.

'I gave her one, they gave him two,
You gave us three or more;

They all returned from him to you,
Though they were mine before.'

'That's the most important piece of evidence we've heard,' said the King.

'It doesn't mean a thing,' said Alice, who had grown so tall in the last few minutes, she wasn't at all afraid of interrupting.

The King peered at the poem. 'There *is* some meaning in it. For instance, the line *"I said I couldn't swim."* '

He turned to the Knave. '*You* can't swim, can you?'

The Knave shook his head sadly. 'Do I look like it?' he said.

The King muttered: 'Then there's the line "I gave her one, they gave him two."'

He looked up.

'That must be what he did with the tarts! Let the jury consider their verdict.'

'No! No!' said the Queen. 'Sentence first – verdict afterwards.'

'That's rubbish,' said Alice, 'the idea of

having the sentence first!'

'Hold your tongue,' said the Queen and she turned purple.

'I won't!' said Alice loudly.

'Off with her head!' the Queen shouted at the top of her voice. But nobody moved.

By this time Alice had grown to her full size. 'Who cares about any of you,' she said, 'you're nothing but a pack of cards!'

At this the whole pack rose up into the air and came flying down on her. Alice screamed and tried to beat them off.

Then, to her surprise, she found herself lying on the grassy bank. Her head was in the lap of her sister, who was gently brushing away some dead leaves that had fluttered down from the trees.

'Come on, wake up!' said her sister. 'You've been asleep for ages!'

Alice yawned and sat up. 'I've had the strangest dream!' she said and began to tell her sister all about her incredible adventures.

Her sister patted her head. 'It's the oddest dream I've ever heard of,' she said. 'But it's getting late now. It's nearly tea-time. We'd better go home.'

Alice got up and ran in front of her sister. She wanted to be on her own for a while, so that she could think about her adventures and all the creatures and people she had met. It was the most amazing dream, she thought. I'll remember it for the rest of my life.